Visit us on the Web! rhcbooks.com

Educators and librarians, for a variety of teaching tools, visit us at RHTeachersLibrarians.com

Library of Congress Cataloging-in-Publication Data
Names: Gilland, Åsa, illustrator.
Title: Welcome to Florida / by Åsa Gilland.
Description: First edition. | New York : Doubleday, [2021] | Audience: Ages 3–7. |
Summary: "An illustrated introduction to the state of Florida" —Provided by publisher.
Identifiers: LCCN 2020010021 (print) | LCCN 2020010022 (ebook)
ISBN 978-0-593-17825-6 (trade) | ISBN 978-0-593-17826-3 (ebook)
Subjects: LCSH: Florida—Juvenile literature.
Classification: LCC F311.3 .G55 2021 (print) | LCC F311.3 (ebook) | DDC 975.9—dc23

MANUFACTURED IN CHINA
10 9 8 7 6 5 4 3 2 1
First Edition

WELCOME to FLORIDA

illustrated by **Åsa Gilland**

Doubleday Books for Young Readers

WELCOME to FLORIDA!

WE'RE GLAD YOU'RE HERE!

ALASKA

WASHINGTON
OREGON
MONTANA
IDAHO
WYOMING
NORTH DAKOTA
SOUTH DAKOTA
MINNESOTA
WISCONSIN
MICHIGAN
NEW YO
NEVADA
CALIFORNIA
UTAH
COLORADO
NEBRASKA
IOWA
ILLINOIS
INDIANA
OHIO
PENNSYLVANIA
WEST VIRGINIA
VIRGINIA
ARIZONA
NEW MEXICO
KANSAS
MISSOURI
KENTUCKY
TENNESSEE
NORTH CAROLINA
OKLAHOMA
ARKANSAS
SOUTH CAROLINA
TEXAS
MISSISSIPPI
ALABAMA
GEORGIA
LOUISIANA
HAWAII
TALLAHASSEE
FLORIDA

MAINE

NEW HAMPSHIRE
MASSACHUSETTS
RHODE ISLAND
CONNECTICUT
NEW JERSEY
AWARE
YLAND

Capital city: Tallahassee
State nickname: The Sunshine State
State motto: "In God we trust"

FLORIDA

Can you guess why Florida is called the Sunshine State?
Florida is bright and sunny all year. Grab your sunglasses
and come see the beautiful beaches, sweet orange groves,
fun theme parks, and incredible wildlife.

JACKSONVILLE

GAINESVILLE

ST. AUGUSTINE

DAYTONA BEACH

CAPE CANAVERAL

ORLANDO

TAMPA

ST. PETERSBURG

SARASOTA

LAKE OKEECHOBEE

ATLANTIC OCEAN

WEST PALM BEACH

CAPE CORAL

BIG CYPRESS SWAMP

MIAMI

THE EVERGLADES

KEY WEST

FLORIDA KEYS

MOCKINGBIRD

The mockingbird is Florida's state bird. It loves to tweet and chirp, and it even sings the songs of other birds and animals!

But don't let that pretty song fool you. It's also a fierce fighter. If an animal or person gets near its nest, the mockingbird will swoop down fast to scare the intruder away.

Florida is famous for its orange trees, and the orange blossom is the state flower. It smells beautiful when it blooms in spring.

ORANGE BLOSSOM

FLORIDA PANTHER

The state animal is the Florida panther. This large wild cat lives in the forests and swamps of southern Florida.

Florida is full of incredible animals! You'll find many beautiful birds near the water, such as flamingos, herons, and pelicans.

FLAMINGO

PELICAN

HERON

The swamps are home to fierce crocodiles and alligators, and gentle manatees live in rivers and lakes.

CROCODILE

FLORIDA ♥

ALLIGATOR

DOLPHIN

MANATEE

You can even see playful dolphins diving in the ocean!

If you love going to the beach, you'll love Florida! It has two main coasts, the Gulf of Mexico and the Atlantic Ocean, and many small islands you can visit.

What would you like to do at the beach?

Florida is a great place to find fresh fruit, tasty seafood, and yummy snacks.

STRAWBERRIES

KEY LIME PIE

STONE CRAB

APALACHICOLA OYSTERS

PASTELITOS

ORANGES

CUBAN SANDWICH

EXTRA HOT
FLORIDA
HOT SAUCE

CONCH FRITTERS

BOILED PEANUTS

WHICH one is your FAVORITE?

Florida is home to many people from Cuba. Little Havana (*Pequeña Habana*) is a Cuban neighborhood in Miami, where you can hear salsa music, play dominoes, and see the Walk of Fame, which honors famous Cuban Americans. You can also eat delicious food such as arroz con pollo, ropa vieja, and plantains.

Have you ever wanted to travel to outer space? The Kennedy Space Center is NASA's main rocket-launch site. The first American in space blasted off from here, and so did the first men who landed on the moon. You can visit and see rockets firing up into the sky!

A great state like Florida has a lot of unusual things to see if you're out for a drive:

MONKEY ISLAND

Who lives on this tiny island with a lighthouse? Monkeys! They love to climb and play on the ropes, and are fed and cared for by the townspeople of Homosassa.

OCHOPEE POST OFFICE

The smallest post office in the United States is a tiny building in the Everglades that was once a storage shed!

SOUTHERNMOST POINT BUOY

If you go all the way to the bottom of Key West, you'll find a buoy that marks the southernmost point in the continental United States. If you kept going south, you would leave the United States and land at the island of Cuba, ninety miles away.

If you love Florida, then you're a Florida kid!
And Florida kids are the best!

Hello!

HEY!

UNITED STATES
AME